IMAGES
of America

SOUTH CAROLINA PORTS
Charleston, Georgetown,
and Port Royal

Charleston's Battery marks the point where, as local tradition tells, "the Cooper and Ashley Rivers meet to form the Atlantic Ocean." (Courtesy Jupiter Images.)

IMAGES
of America

SOUTH CAROLINA PORTS
*Charleston, Georgetown,
and Port Royal*

Shelia Hempton Watson

ARCADIA
PUBLISHING

Published by Arcadia Publishing
Charleston, South Carolina

Library of Congress Catalog Card Number: 2004108901

For all general information contact Arcadia Publishing at:
Telephone 843-853-2070
Fax 843-853-0044
E-mail sales@arcadiapublishing.com
For customer service and orders:
Toll-Free 1-888-313-2665

Visit us on the Internet at www.arcadiapublishing.com

Even as early as 1762, steeples defined Charleston's skyline as seen from the harbor. (Courtesy Jupiter Images.)

CONTENTS

ACKNOWLEDGMENTS

Telling the story of the ports of South Carolina is a delight, yet it is not a story one could tell alone. The area is simply too big and the tale too intricate for one voice or one vision. Many people deserve thanks for their contributions and assistance on this project.

My appreciation goes first to Marion Bull, manager of publications, marketing, and research, and Marvin Preston, photographer extraordinaire, both colleagues of mine working on the State Ports Authority's magazine, *PortCharleston*. Reminiscences and insights from several other staff members as well as records and documents from the Ports Authority contributed significantly to the narrative. In particular, I acknowledge the story contained in *History of South Carolina State Ports Authority*, coordinated by Anne M. Moise and the Public Relations division of the Ports Authority.

I am grateful for assistance from Patrick Cook at Charles Towne Landing and Al Hester at the South Carolina Department of Parks, Recreation, and Tourism. A thank you is due also to Bunky Wichmann and DuBose Blakeney for assistance above and beyond in obtaining certain photos. Brad and Meaghan Van Liew and the South Carolina Maritime Heritage Foundation were generous with assistance, as was Dr. Jonathan Leader of the South Carolina Institute of Archaeology and Anthropology at the University of South Carolina. All was greatly appreciated.

For assistance in research and collecting certain images, thanks go out to Jane Yates of the Citadel Archives & Museum office, Theresa Roberts of the U.S. Coast Guard historian's office, Mike Coker of the South Carolina Historical Society, and Tom Spain of the *Post and Courier*'s photography staff.

The history of South Carolina's ports is an intriguing tale, especially told in this visual format. This book is in no way meant to be an exhaustive account of Charleston, Georgetown, and Port Royal. Rather, my intention was to provide enough of a glimpse of the story to evoke further interest in the rich maritime heritage of South Carolina's ports.

About the photos:
Unless otherwise noted, all photos are courtesy the South Carolina State Ports Authority or are in the public domain. Certain images in this book are the copyrighted property of Jupiter Images and are being used with permission under license.

FOREWORD

This book provides a window to the images of South Carolina's history in maritime trade and defense. It is a wonderful pictorial account of more than 300 years of the state's three port cities and the role they have played in its development.

Charleston, Georgetown, and Port Royal became port cities because of their strategic positions along South Carolina's coast and the Atlantic's shores. They have each over time provided protected harbors for commercial vessels as well as battleships, making South Carolina a crossroads of international commerce and U.S. defense. Though the Charleston Naval Base and Shipyard closed after almost 100 years of operation, the area still plays a critical role in military deployments, training, technology, and national security. And the state's waterborne commerce has shifted from a reliance on exports of cotton, indigo, and rice in Colonial times to achieving the current status of being the fourth largest containerport in the United States.

It is a privilege to be associated with the South Carolina State Ports Authority and to have had the opportunity to experience the rapid growth of our public ports. Our mission is clear: to promote economic growth by facilitating international trade. But in addition to a healthier economy, global trade has also brought the added benefit of cultural diversity to South Carolina. This positive change is evident as you peruse the photographs in this book.

Our ports will continue to evolve. Future change will come with new cargo handling technologies, with shifts in global trading patterns, with national security requirements, and with consumer demand. In any case, South Carolina's ports will continue to be a key to its economic success.

Bernard S. Groseclose Jr.

INTRODUCTION

When eight English noblemen known as the Lords Proprietors were granted the Charles Towne territory by King Charles II, the grant came with an express command: go forth and develop the area into a profit-making venture. Fortunately, the area came with a natural deep-water port, perfect for establishing trade.

Soon, trade in a variety of goods established Charles Towne's wealth and prosperity. The invention of the cotton gin and improvements in the rice crop cultivation ("cotton was king and rice was gold" was the saying) were a boost to Charleston's economy. By 1750, Charleston was the fourth largest city in Colonial America and the wealthiest. Charleston Harbor served as a major shipping port for the rice and indigo produced throughout the region, and it was the first port to receive slaves.

By 1729, Georgetown was a busy seaport as well, with imports and exports that created incredible wealth for the settlers of the area.

Port Royal is perhaps one of the most resilient and flexible areas in the South. After her founding in 1521, she saw seven flags fly over her port before Old Glory finally took command. Before long, Port Royal was known far and wide as an important shipbuilding facility.

During the Civil War, Charleston's port served as a lifeline to the Confederacy. In order to block the shipments of food, medicine, and other supplies coming in, the Union Navy blockaded the harbor by sinking several large ships in the harbor. Among the efforts to retaliate was the sinking of the Union ship *Housatonic* by the Confederate submarine *H.L. Hunley*, which itself sank. The *Hunley* was raised in 2000 and is now on display at a facility on the former U.S. Navy base.

After the Civil War, the plantation system collapsed, and Charleston struggled with a shattered economy. With the establishment of the Charleston Naval Shipyard during World War I and several military-related industries during World War II, the harbor came alive, and Charleston began to thrive again.

In the 1940s, the State established the State Ports Authority to manage the ports of Charleston, Georgetown, and Port Royal. The mission of the State Ports Authority is to "contribute to the economic development of South Carolina by fostering and stimulating waterborne commerce and shipment of freight," a mission it continues to fulfill.

The 1960s saw the onset of containerization, which revolutionized cargo shipments and gave a needed boost to South Carolina's economy. Port Charleston has grown into one of the busiest ports in the Southeast and one of the largest containerized cargo ports on the South Atlantic and Gulf coasts. Some 2,100 ships come in and out of Charleston's port each year, an average of about six per day. Today, Charleston remains a significant seaport. Ranked fourth in container shipments, Charleston is distinguished as the second most efficient seaport in the world (after Hong Kong.)

The value of South Carolina's ports to national security is also well documented. Despite the closing of the naval base in 1995, much of the mobilization of troops and supplies is staged at the North Charleston terminal through the Military Traffic Management Command. In fact, all training for MTMC's personnel (who work in a dozen different locations nationwide) occurs at the Charleston facility.

In addition, the border patrol, customs officials, coast guard, and other maritime security personnel are trained in Charleston. Since September 11, maritime security has become an even greater priority. Charleston's importance is highlighted by the Department of Homeland Security's choice of Port Charleston as the pilot site for Project Seahawk. The nation's first port security command and control center, Project Seahawk is a comprehensive effort to coordinate the port security responsibilities of the various federal, state, local, and private entities charged with defending the Port of Charleston. Project Seahawk brings together agencies such as the Federal Bureau of Investigation, Immigration and Naturalization Service, U.S. Customs Service, U.S. Coast Guard, Transportation Security Administration, South Carolina Law Enforcement Division, and the State Ports Authority under one port security command center. This unique intermodal transportation and port security pilot project began in Charleston in March 2003 and will set the course for port security nationwide.

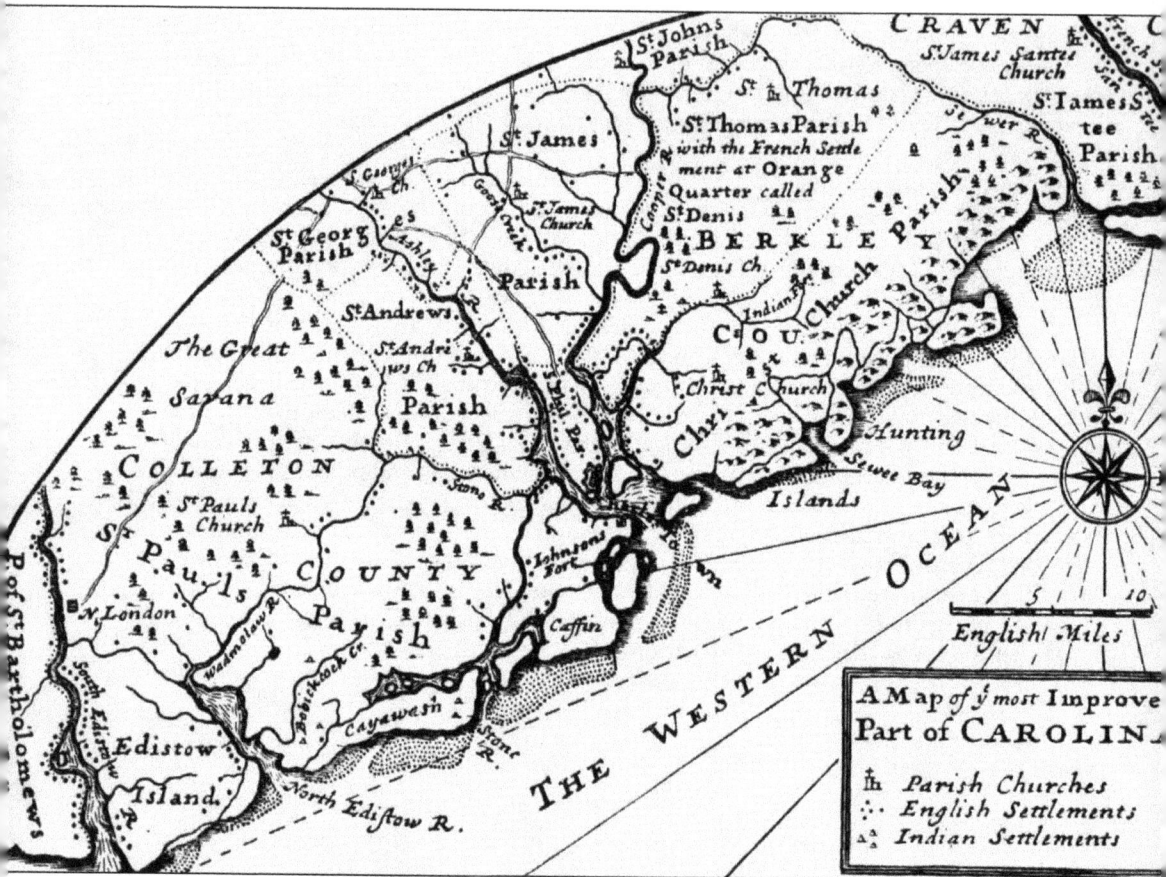

This c. 1742 map of the "Most Improved Part of Carolina" shows the accessibility of the state's ports. By the 1700s, Charleston, Georgetown, and Port Royal were established and prosperous enough to attract others looking for a fast path to wealth: settlers, investors, and pirates. (Courtesy Jupiter Images.)

One

NATURAL
DEEP-WATER HARBORS

The history of South Carolina's ports begins in the 16th century, when explorers arrived in the area and found a land inhabited by several small tribes of Native Americans. The first European attempts at settlement—one in 1526 by Spanish explorers at Winyah Bay (Georgetown) and one in 1562 by French Huguenots led by Jean Ribaut at Port Royal—failed.

The third time was a charm, with the establishment of an English colony in 1670 at Albemarle Point on the west bank of the Ashley River. Granted the territory by King Charles II as a reward for loyalty, the Lords Proprietors of Carolina promptly named it Charles Towne and began the task of making money for the king.

While the high ground at Albemarle Point offered a good vantage point for spotting enemies approaching by sea, the shallow creek leading to the landing could accommodate only a few ships at a time, which made the site impractical. To enhance trade, Charles Towne was moved in 1680 to Oyster Point on the peninsula between the Ashley and Cooper Rivers (originally named, respectively, the Kiawah and Wando Rivers). The new site was able to accommodate a larger number of ships, and trade in several commodities, particularly rice and indigo, soon marked Charles Towne as a prosperous locale.

Among those who took notice of the prosperity were pirates. The most notable of these, Edward Teach, also known as Blackbeard, frequented the waterways of Georgetown. Other pirates stirred up trouble in Port Royal. Charleston saw the execution of many of them.

During the Civil War, Charleston was not only the place where hostilities began, but also a lifeline to the Confederacy. Eventually, the Union Navy blockaded the harbor and cut the supply link. After the war, Charleston struggled to deal with a broken economy. Help finally arrived with the establishment of a large naval shipyard during World War I and several military-related industries during World War II.

Early ships used cobblestone for ballast, which were removed from the ships and used to pave some of the downtown streets, such as Gillon Street, next to the Exchange Building.

The U.S. Customs House flanked by church steeples prove this image to be unmistakably Charleston Harbor. (Courtesy Jupiter Images.)

This statue of Chief Cassique of the Kiawah Indians is displayed at Charles Towne Landing, the location of the original settlement. Cassique's tribe was instrumental in helping the early settlers establish the colony. (Photo from the author's collection. Courtesy South Carolina Parks, Recreation, and Tourism.)

Although this c. 1700 map of Charleston Harbor shows the peninsula somewhat misshapen, the map accurately depicts the location of Old Charles Towne (present-day Charles Towne Landing), Sullivan's Island, and Wappoo Creek. (Courtesy Jupiter Images.)

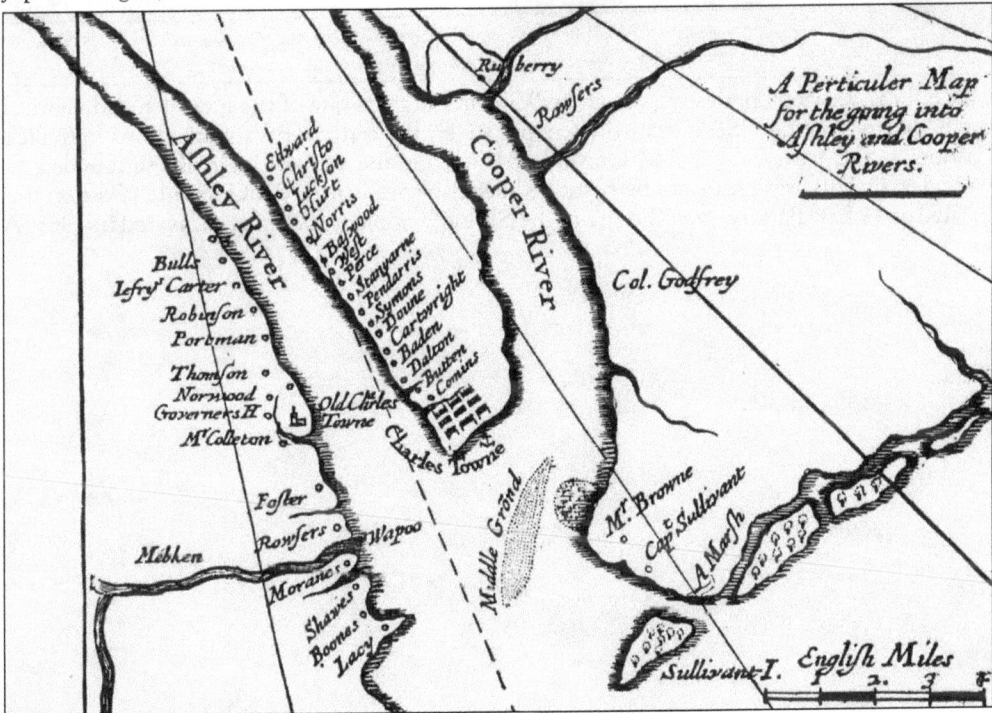

his Excellency James Glen Esq. Capt. General, Governor, & Commander in Chief in, and over his MAJESTY'S Province of South Carolina, and Vice Admiral within the Same. This Prospect of CHARLES TOWN is most humbly Inscribed by his much Obliged humble Servant B: Roberts.

This *c.* 1737 view of Charleston, drawn by William Burgis, is one of the most detailed views of the early Colonial city. Seen from the Cooper River, the waterfront is marked by Granville's Bastion at the extreme left and Craven's Bastion on the right. Originally surrounded by palisades, the city was protected by bastioned defensive walls in 1701. Granville's Bastion was located at 44 East Battery, now the site of the Shrine Temple, which was excavated in 1925. A

low tabby seawall just to the south is all that remains. Craven's Bastion was located at the east end of Market Street on the Cooper River. Remnants were uncovered during the building of the U.S. Customs House in the late 19th century. Other visible landmarks include St. Philip's Church on the skyline. (Courtesy Historic Urban Plans, Ithaca, New York.)

This sketch of Charleston, published in *Frank Leslie's Illustrated Newspaper*, December 8, 1860, depicts a general view of the harbor just before the onset of the Civil War. The detail (shown opposite page, bottom) reveals the telltale Charleston steeples. (Courtesy The Citadel Archives & Museum.)

Since Columbus discovered America in 1492, seven flags have flown over what is now known as Port Royal. The port town was under the control of (from left to right, beginning on the top row) Spain (1521–1587), France (1562), England (1670–1776), Scotland (1684), America following the Revolution (1777), South Carolina before the Civil War (1861), and the Confederacy during the Civil War (1861–1865).

The tidelands of Georgetown were ideal for growing two of the most valuable crops in the new world—indigo (left) and rice. Trading in Georgetown indigo created fortunes that rivaled the wealth of the royalty of Europe. Around 1680, rice seeds were brought into the port of Charleston from Madagascar. By the late 1700s, some of the cypress swamps in Georgetown County were cleared, canals were dug, and the second largest rice culture in the world was established. Two varieties—"Carolina Gold" and "Waccamaw Gold"—were sought by grocers in England. This singular crop sustained the economy of Georgetown for more than a century.

Georgetown's wealth didn't escape the notice of pirates such as Blackbeard (Edward Teach). He haunted the coastline of Carolina for years in his ship *Queen Anne's Revenge*.

In the years before the American Revolution, Charleston was the fourth largest city in the colonies and easily the wealthiest. As such, she was a coveted prize for the British. (Courtesy Jupiter Images.)

PLAN OF THE SEIGE OF **CHARLESTON** IN S. CAROLINA

SCALE OF 2500 YARDS

HARPER'S WEEKLY

A JOURNAL OF CIVILIZATION.

Vol. VI.—No. 263.]   NEW YORK, SATURDAY, JANUARY 11, 1862.   [SINGLE COPIES SIX CENTS. / $2.50 PER YEAR IN ADVANCE.

Entered according to Act of Congress, in the Year 1862, by Harper & Brothers, in the Clerk's Office of the District Court for the Southern District of New York.

The caption from this cover of *Harper's Weekly* on January 11, 1982, reads, "Sinking the Stone Fleet in Charleston Harbor." The image depicts the deliberate sinking of several ships in Charleston Harbor by the Union Navy in an attempt to blockade Confederate shipping. (Courtesy The Citadel Archives & Museum.)

This *c.* 1890 photo shows some of the wharves in Charleston at low tide. (From the Weston family collection, courtesy Bunky Wichmann.)

This *c.* 1890 photo shows a view of Charleston Harbor, including several tall ships, from a dock on the Ashley River. (From the Weston family collection, courtesy Bunky Wichmann.)

Wharves on the Cooper River are shown in this *c.* 1890 photo. Note the line of tall ships in the background. (From the Weston family collection, courtesy Bunky Wichmann.)

This is Charleston Harbor as seen from St. Michael's Church *c.* 1890. (From the Weston family collection, courtesy Bunky Wichmann.)

Two

Trade Routes
and Cargo

With a command from the king to develop Carolina into a profit-making center, the early colonists looked around for items to trade. With the rich soil and tidal basins at their disposal, the colonists didn't have to look far. They bartered with the Native Americans, trading trinkets and cloth for animal pelts, which were sent to furriers and hatmakers in Europe.

By the mid-1670s, meat and lumber were traded to the West Indies for rum and sugar. Shipbuilding materials were sent to England in exchange for English-manufactured goods. In 1683, one settler remarked that "the port is never without ships and the country is becoming a great traffic center."

By the mid-1700s, the South Carolina coast had become a bustling trade center, and one of the primary crops was cotton. In fact, the saying "cotton was king" was generally considered a fact of life. In 1764, the customhouse in London recorded a shipment of eight bales of cotton from Charles Towne—the first transatlantic cotton shipment on record.

Another profitable cash crop was rice. Demand for the product was greatest in northern Europe, and by the 1720s, most of the value of the colony's exports came from rice. About 1740, indigo became an important staple of trade for the colony, exported primarily out of Georgetown.

Slave trade from Africa to Carolina also flourished and would do so until the Civil War. From 1716 to 1808, Charleston was the port of entry for more than 20 percent of all slaves brought into America.

Charleston was a primary trade route destination for European ships, and many commodities made their way to Europe via South Carolina's ports. In 1773, the *South Carolina Gazette* ran a story about the 125-ton ship *Live Oak*, which was "constantly employed in the Trade between this Port and Europe." (The vessel, incidentally, had been built on James Island 24 years before.)

After the Revolutionary War, Charleston, Georgetown, and Port Royal became more prosperous in the plantation-dominated economy. The invention of the cotton gin in 1793 revolutionized production. Cotton quickly became South Carolina's major export and remained so until the late 1820s, when cotton from Western states glutted the market.

After the Civil War, which all but devastated the area, phosphate trade was important to both Port Royal and Charleston. Georgetown exported large quantities of lumber products to the Northeast.

By the 20th century, South Carolina was starting to recover economically. The textile industry began to develop and expand, and trade soon picked up with a wide variety of bulk cargoes.

Although port activity in Charleston, Georgetown, and Port Royal has been somewhat of an ebb and flood over the years, trade through South Carolina has never halted altogether. Cargo moving through the state's ports composes quite a list. From ice (the first commercial transport by ship came from New York to Charleston in 1799), chickens, and flour to sulphur, rolled steel, and lumber to boats, cars, and huge generators, South Carolina's ports have seen it all come through.

A bell for the Citadel's carillon arrives in Charleston in August 1954.

Pineapple from Hawaii is one of the imports coming through the port of Charleston c. 1952.

At the North Charleston terminal, lumber is loaded on a ship bound for Puerto Rico. A housing boom on the Caribbean island in the early 1950s raised exports of lumber.

Steel from Belgium arrives in Charleston on the vessel *Southstar* in January 1951.

Trade with Japan was going strong in October 1957 when this shipment of plywood was exported through Charleston.

Tall oil, a chemical by-product manufactured by the Charleston plant of West Virginia Pulp and Paper Company, is loaded onto a ship at the North Charleston terminal for shipment abroad.

Bags of flour are stacked in one of the Ports Authority's warehouses to await export.

The docks at Port Royal are kept busy with import and export of bulk products.

In a June 1960 shipment, Southern Shipping Company loaded 400 tons of chicken onto the SS *Cabo Frio* for West Germany, Holland, and Switzerland.

A shipment of peanuts, *c.* 1950, makes its way from the fields in neighboring Georgia to the Charleston waterfront and onto a vessel bound for European connoisseurs who relish this "caviar of the South."

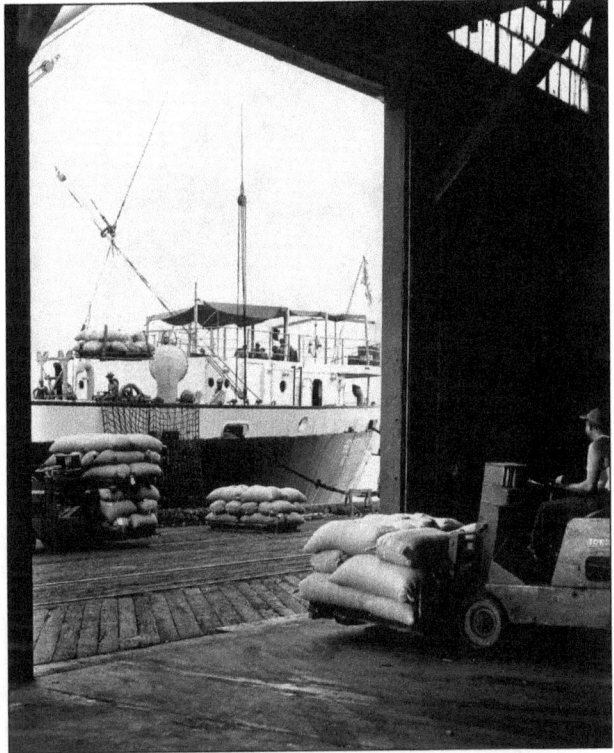

Barbed wire and fencing, imported from Europe, is offloaded at the North Charleston terminal in the 1950s.

By the 1950s, textiles were the leading exports moving through South Carolina's ports. Before World War II, textiles moved primarily through Northern ports.

In the late 1940s and early 1950s, foreign wool was a brand new import cargo for the port of Charleston. After offloading, the shipments were sent to the large combing plants—the Prouvost plant at Jamestown and the Wellman plant at Johnsonville.

Paper products loaded onto outbound ships are a common site at each of the terminals in Charleston, Georgetown, and Port Royal.

Judging by the script on the sides of the containers, these chemical exports are shipping to the Middle East.

Export steel has been a rare commodity in the past, but an improvement in the export market in recent years has resulted in an increase in steel coil shipments through the port. In one month, two shipments totaling 55,000 tons were exported from Nucor Steel, located on the upper reaches of the Cooper River.

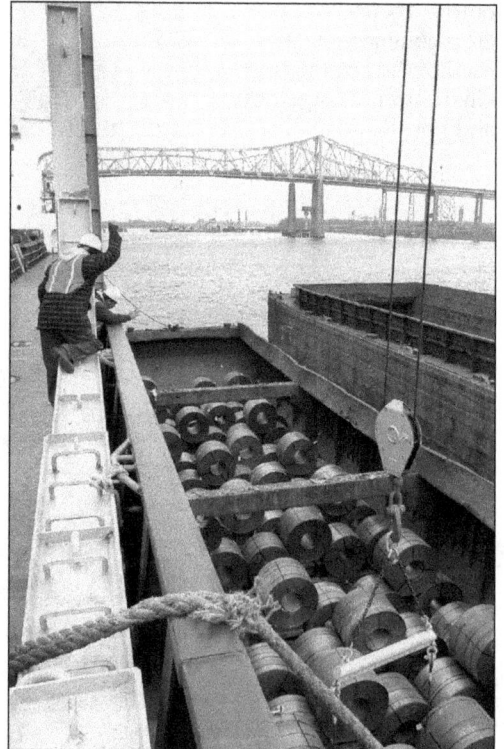

Nucor is a major importer of bulk pig iron, hot briquette iron, and scrap iron used to feed its large steel mill. Nucor works barges from its own dock and crane facility. The barge is moored at shipside, where the ship's gear lifts the coils onto the vessel.

These c. 1950s photos show sulphur, one of the leading bulk products, being processed through the port. The scoop digs deep into the hold of the ship (above) and drops the load onto the railcars (below).

The port's 400-ton derrick (affectionately called "The Monster") easily handles a fertilizer plant component weighing more than 300 tons. It was one of 50 major pieces of a 2,943-ton heavy-lift shipment. Three ocean-going barges brought the material to Charleston, and 20 flatbed motor carriers were needed to move it inland to its destination.

A specialized hauler is lowered into the hold of a cargo ship. Heavy-lift cranes make the job look easy.

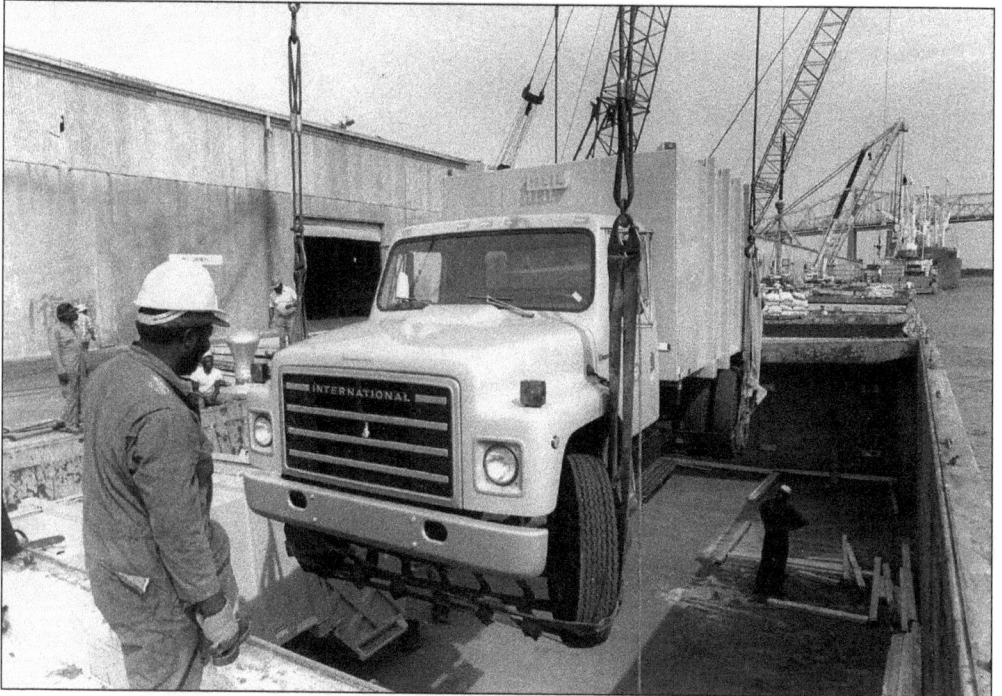

Cargo of all shapes and sizes moves through the port, but a locomotive being lifted aboard a vessel is certainly among the more unusual. This shipment is headed to Korea c. 1960s.

This International Harvester pay hauler is loaded onto the freighter Ocean Victory at the North Charleston terminal in May 1961. The ship set sail for the Mediterranean.

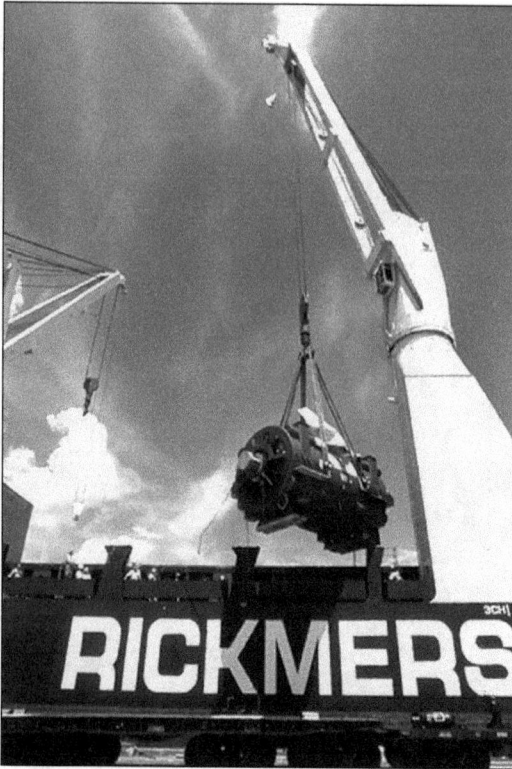

In this 2002 cargo project, several large pieces of equipment were imported from Japan to the United States for a power generator plant in North Carolina. The pieces were unusually heavy—a 269,000-pound turbine engine and a 567,000-pound generator—and were loaded directly onto the railcar at the ship's side at the Columbus Street Terminal. The equipment was brought to Charleston by Rickmers, a breakbulk specialty carrier.

This boat loading onto the vessel *Whirlwind* looks like a game of very heavy piggyback. The boat was a *c.* 1960s export to Europe, where she no doubt ended up cruising the Mediterranean.

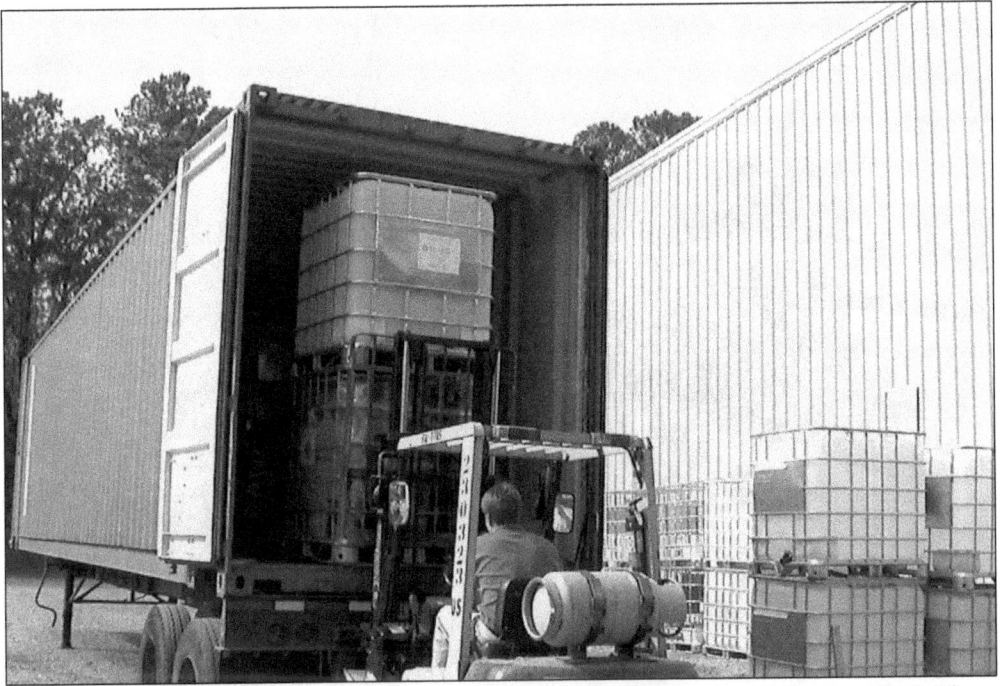

The port sometimes has the opportunity to ship products used for humanitarian relief. These water treatment units are manufactured by Water Missions International, located in Charleston, and shipped to areas around the world where unclean water is a health threat. Several units (above) are loaded onto a container and readied for shipment. Among those receiving WMI's water treatment units are the people of Afghanistan (below).

Special vessels are used for Ro/Ro (roll-on/roll-off) cargo—that is, cargo that can move onto the vessel on its own wheels instead of being lifted by cranes. Here, a delivery of John Deere tractors is lined up in front of a Ro/Ro ship. Below, a trailer enables a Ro/Ro shipment of boats.

The world's largest fire truck is shown in this February 1981 photo rolling on board a ship at the Columbus Street Terminal for export to the Middle East. The 78,000-pound vehicle was built specifically for aircraft firefighting and rescue work.

This Ro/Ro vessel is taking on bulk cargo—plywood from Georgia Pacific Company in Georgetown—via forklifts.

Among the more luxurious Ro/Ro cargo shipments are the BMW vehicles that cover the lot at Columbus Street Terminal waiting for export. The cars are shipped by rail directly to the terminal from the BMW plant in Upstate South Carolina. BMW is a significant factor in the

state's economy. In 2003, BMW and its suppliers shipped more than half a billion pounds of cargo through Charleston. To support production at its Greer plant, BMW imported more than 3,800 containers of parts and components.

Shrink-wrapped BMWs arrive in Charleston and head out via Ro/Ro to Southampton, England, and Bremerhaven, Germany.

Containerization has revolutionized shipping in unusual ways. One port customer imports his cargo—restored classic Mini cars—in containers. Because the cars are so compact, a container can hold up to seven of them. The seller, a resident of England, packs the container and meets the ship two weeks later in Charleston.

Three

SHIPYARDS AND SHIPBUILDING

For many of the early settlers, the trip across the ocean was a ghastly experience, with months of rough seas, bad food, and sickness. As soon as they had recovered long enough to settle into their homes, they turned their attention, naturally, to boatbuilding.

One such instance was an act of desperation. In 1563, a small group of French Huguenot settlers, who had been left behind in Port Royal by their leader, Jean Ribaut, set sail for home in a makeshift vessel they built—the first American-built ship to sail the Atlantic. Their vessel floundered at sea, but they were picked up by English sailors and returned to France.

For others in the colony, boats and ships were a way of life. Deep-draft European ships were impractical for the shallow waters of the sea islands, so the settlers learned from the Native Americans how to build dugout crafts from cypress trees. Schooners were used for coastal transport and trading, although not for transatlantic voyages.

As the colony grew, so did the shipbuilding industry, which soon became South Carolina's largest manufacturing industry. Early ship registers reveal that more than 300 ocean-going and coastal cargo vessels were built by South Carolina shipbuilders between 1735 and 1775. The shipbuilding sites were located along many of South Carolina's rivers, such as those at Dewees Island, Combahee, Wadmalaw, Pocotaligo, and Bull's Island. The major shipbuilding areas were in Charleston, Georgetown, and the most important at Port Royal. In the Charleston area, most shipbuilding took place at James Island, Shipyard Creek, and Hobcaw.

The Revolutionary War adversely affected shipbuilding at Port Royal, a fate from which it never recovered. By the 1800s, South Carolina could not compete with New England's shipbuilding industry, and by the mid-1800s, the development of steamships and steel-hulled vessels cut wooden shipbuilding almost entirely.

Shipbuilding in South Carolina had a revival of sorts when the Charleston Naval Shipyard was founded in 1901. The shipyard continued to grow during both World Wars and became the major industry in the area.

In July 1993, the Base Realignment and Closure Commission (BRAC) voted to close the naval base and shipyard. Several small shipyards and drydocks remain in the area, but with the closing, Charleston's influence as a major shipbuilding force was diminished.

Tall ships often pay a visit to historic Charleston. Here, one holds a grand pose while modern speedboats circle for a closer look.

The *Carolina*, largest of the three vessels that brought the original English settlers, is described as a frigate of about 200 tons. She carried 92 passengers with a crew of 19 and was armed with 16 "great guns." Of the three original vessels, she was the only one to reach her destination, the *Albemarle* and the *Port Royal* having been replaced during the voyage. This half-inch scale model was researched and designed by William A. Baker, a naval architect of Hingham, Massachusetts, and built by Erik A.R. Ronnberg Jr. of South Dartmouth, Massachusetts. The model is on display at Charles Towne Landing. (Courtesy South Carolina Parks, Recreation, and Tourism.)

The *Adventure* is a life-size reproduction of a typical trading ship of the 17th century docked on Old Town Creek at Charles Towne Landing. The full-scale reproduction emphasizes the important role trade played in the development of the colony. (Courtesy South Carolina Parks, Recreation, and Tourism.)

In building the reproduction, craftsmanship is a key element—as true today as it would have been in the 1600s. (Courtesy South Carolina Parks, Recreation, and Tourism.)

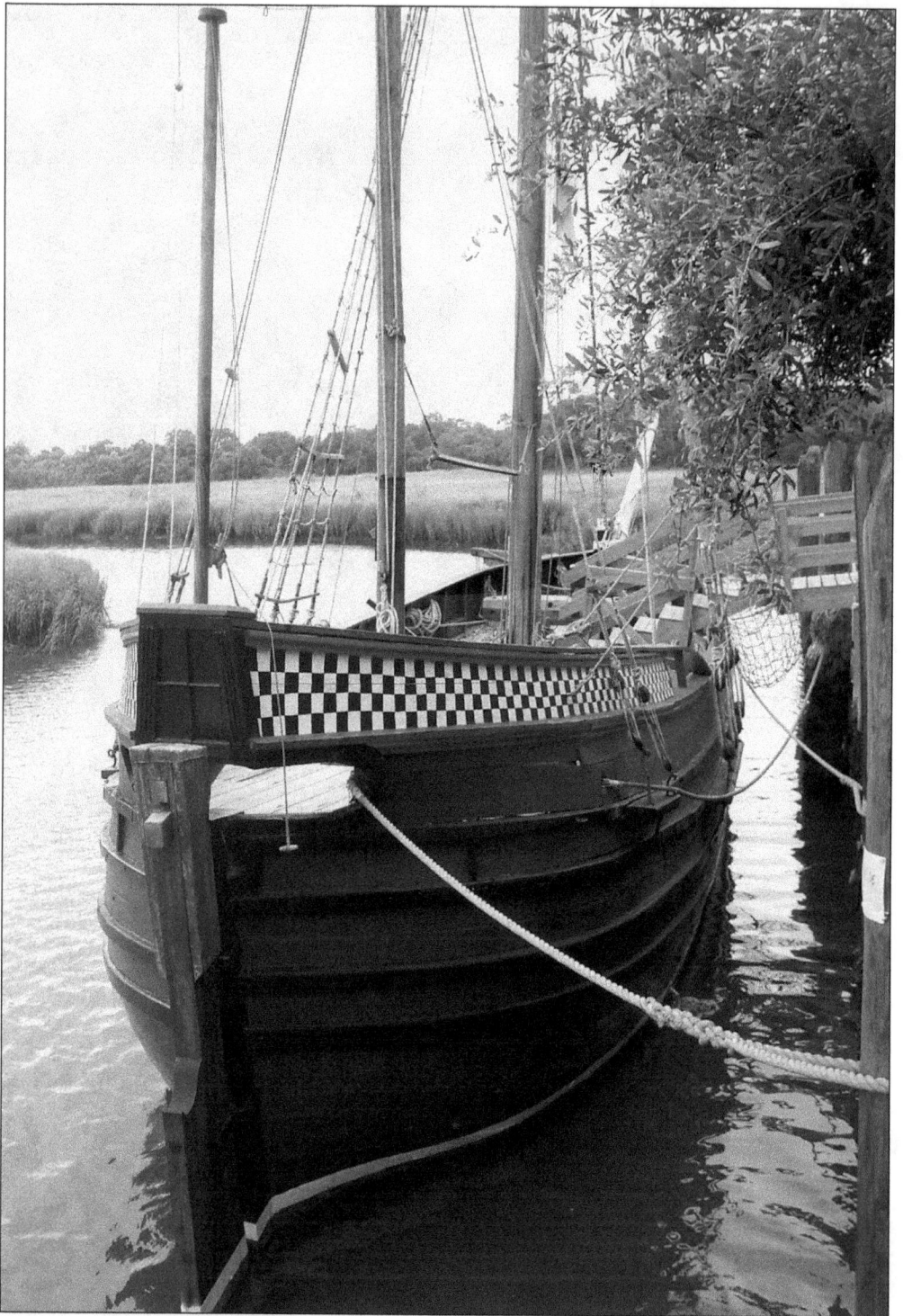

The *Adventure* was designed to be a cargo vessel that would carry supplies, provisions, commodities, and livestock between New Amsterdam (present New York) and Barbados in the West Indies. (Photo from the author's collection.)

The *Adventure* was designed by renowned 20th-century shipwright William A. Baker in 1969 and set underway in March 1970 to celebrate the tricentennial at Charles Towne Landing in April 1970. (Courtesy South Carolina Parks, Recreation, and Tourism.)

The South Carolina Maritime Heritage Foundation has undertaken the building of a tall ship, named the *Spirit of South Carolina*, which will provide educational opportunities and sailing experience primarily for youth. The shipyard, located on property loaned from the City at Ansonborough Field (shown above), will be a "living museum" for the duration of the project, offering a chance to observe and interact with maritime and shipbuilding history in the making. Plans for the ship were found in the Smithsonian Institution ship plans collection. The ship (whose partially finished hull is shown below) is being built traditionally from recycled live oak, white oak, and long-leaf yellow pine. (Photo above by Debra Gingrich, courtesy the South Carolina Maritime Heritage Foundation. Photo below by Marvin Preston, courtesy the South Carolina State Ports Authority.)

A model of the *Spirit of South Carolina* was built by Bill Baum (shown below). Upon completing the model, he remarked, "The project initiated by the South Carolina Maritime Heritage Foundation seemed worthy of the challenge, namely to build a visual image for potential contributors to justify their involvement." (Photos by Charlie Sneed, courtesy the South Carolina Maritime Heritage Foundation.)

The *Spirit of South Carolina* will be a pilot schooner reminiscent of the 1870s pilot schooner *Frances Elizabeth*, shown in this c. 1889 photo. The *Frances Elizabeth* was originally built by the Samuel J. Pregnall & Bros. Shipyard on what is now the north end of the Union Pier Terminal. (Courtesy the South Carolina Maritime Heritage Foundation.)

Charleston is often host to tall ships, a role the city plays well considering her long history of shipbuilding. Here, two tall ships dock at the Union Pier Terminal during the annual Charleston Maritime Festival.

A similar tall ship project to the *Spirit of South Carolina*, the *Amistad* is a reproduction topsail schooner constructed by Mystic Seaport. Charleston was one of the select sites to host the freedom schooner *Amistad* in its mission to promote reconciliation among races through visits to ports nationally and internationally. The ship was conceived, built, and launched to celebrate the legacy of the Amistad Incident of 1839, in which 53 Africans were kidnapped and sold into slavery. The ship is a "floating classroom" and monument to the lives lost in slave trade. John Kamara (shown below), a native of Freetown, Sierra Leone, displays a model of the *Amistad*.

The USS *Houston*, pictured in drydock at Charleston in May 1917, was the ex-German *Liebenfels*, which had been seized by customs officials in April 1917. (U.S. Navy photograph.)

This *c.* 1950 photo shows the Charleston Naval Shipyard in her heyday. It was established in 1901, and throughout the two World Wars and during most of the Cold War, much of the city's economy relied on the naval defense industry.

On May 21, 1945, the Charleston Shipbuilding and Drydock Company was presented the coveted U.S. Army-Navy E for excellence pennant and E lapel pins. The award was given to government and private production plants that performed exceptional work for the war effort. Only about four percent of plants in the country were similarly honored. The commanding officers for each of the military forces represented in Charleston were present. Charleston mayor E. Edward Wehman Jr. presided over the ceremony. (Official U.S. Coast Guard photograph, courtesy U.S. Coast Guard historian's office.)

The USS *Hubbard* DE-211 (left) and the USS *Hayter* DE-212 are shown at the *Hubbard's* commissioning ceremony March 6, 1944, at Charleston Naval Shipyard. Both were laid down August 11, 1943, and launched November 11, 1943. The *Hayter* was commissioned March 16, 1944. These were only two of dozens of ships launched from Charleston during World War II. (U.S. Navy photograph.)

On July 10, 1939, the day of Sec. Claude Swanson's funeral, the navy department announced that a destroyer would be named for the secretary. The ship was allocated for construction at Charleston Naval Shipyard and expected to be completed in late 1941. In fact, the USS *Swanson* was launched November 2, 1940, and commissioned May 29, 1941. (U.S. Navy photograph.)

The USS *Tidewater* launches at Charleston Naval Shipyard June 30, 1945. (U.S. Navy photograph.)

Four

THE CLARION CALL

When it comes to anteing up during wartime, South Carolina is usually first with the chips.

Charles Towne played a large role in the deteriorating relationship between England and the colonists. While Boston held her "tea party," the tea in Charles Towne was confiscated and stored in the Exchange Building. Representatives came to the Exchange in 1774 to elect delegates to the Continental Congress, a group that was responsible for drafting the Declaration of Independence. Always a step ahead, South Carolina declared her independence from the crown on the steps of the Exchange.

The first major naval battle of the Revolutionary War was fought in the harbor on June 28, 1776. Col. William Moultrie and his patriot troops defeated Sir Peter Parker's attempt to sail a British fleet into the harbor at Charles Towne. They achieved this victory in part due to a hastily constructed palmetto fort, later named Fort Moultrie, on Sullivan's Island. By 1780, the city came under British control for two and a half years. After the British left in December 1782, the city's name was officially changed to Charleston.

Port Royal also saw her share of action. Captain Barnwell held back a British attack on Port Royal in 1779. Fort Lyttleton was built on the site of the former Stuart Town settlement and commanded by William Harden, who organized volunteer artillery now known as the 1055th Transportation Company. The 1055th has seen service in every U.S. war and is the fifth oldest military company in the nation.

In 1860, South Carolina again stepped up to the plate first with the Order of Secession. In January 1861, Citadel cadets fired the first shots of the Civil War when they opened fire on a Union ship entering the harbor. In April of that year, shore batteries under the command of Gen. Pierre G.T. Beauregard opened fire on Union-held Fort Sumter. After Maj. Robert Anderson surrendered the fort to the Confederates, it became a center for blockade running.

The first submarine battle took place in Charleston Harbor with the sinking of the USS *Housatonic* by the Confederate submarine *H.L. Hunley* on February 17, 1864.

After the war, Port Royal benefited from the establishment of a naval and coaling dock built on nearby Parris Island in 1891. Parris Island is home to the U.S. Marines training facility.

From World War II on, the Charleston Navy Yard became a part of the region's livelihood. In the 1960s, the number of military personnel stationed in or near Charleston almost doubled. However, the region's military presence began to decrease in 1989 as the Department of Defense cut military budgets nationally.

Despite the closure of the shipyard and navy base in 1995, the Department of Defense has remained a large part of the region's economy, employing thousands of active duty and civilian personnel at the Charleston Air Force Base, various naval facilities still in the region, and other Department of Defense installations.

During both Operation Desert Storm and Operation Enduring Freedom, Charleston helped the war efforts by loading large supply ships with military cargo. Several independent contractors that manufacture military supplies are located in Charleston, many of them on the site of the former navy base. In addition, the Naval Weapons Station, the Naval Brig, and the military's primary technology center, the Space and Naval Warfare Command Center (SPAWAR), are located in Charleston.

As the setting for the beginning of the Civil War, Fort Sumter is one of the most famous of Charleston's landmarks.

This drawing shows the fortifications of Charles Towne on Albemarle Point (at present-day Charles Towne Landing) as they might have looked in 1670–1671. (Illustration by Darby Erd, courtesy South Carolina Parks, Recreation, and Tourism.)

This engraving from *Harper's Weekly*, May 2, 1963, is captioned "The Defenses of Charleston Looking Seaward." The view is from the Battery. Notice Fort Sumter in the center of the picture. (Courtesy The Citadel Archives & Museum.)

This engraving, captioned "Charleston from Fort Johnson," ran in *Harper's Weekly* on May 2, 1863. The harbor is crowded with vessels of all sizes, from rowboats to tall ships to ironclads. (Courtesy The Citadel Archives & Museum.)

The caption on this engraving from *Frank Leslie's Illustrated Newspaper* of April 25, 1863, reads, "The Advance upon Charleston—Pioneer Movement—Landing of the 100th N.Y. Vol. upon Cole's Island, March 28." (Courtesy The Citadel Archives & Museum.)

The Confederate submersible *H.L. Hunley* was not the nation's first submarine, but it was the first to engage and sink a warship, the USS *Housatonic*. The *Hunley* was designed to be hand-powered by a crew of nine (eight to turn the hand-cranked propeller and one to steer). After achieving her mission to sink the *Housatonic* on the night of February 17, 1864, the *Hunley* sank off the coast of Charleston. She was found 131 years later by famed author Clive Cussler and raised on August 8, 2000. The *Hunley* is housed in the Lasch Conservation Lab located on the former navy base.

This photograph was taken April 14, 1865, during the flag re-raising ceremony at Fort Sumter. Commemorating the four-year anniversary of the surrender of the Union forces at Fort Sumter, Maj. Robert Anderson, who took down the flag in 1861, came back to re-raise the flag. (Official U.S. Coast Guard photograph, courtesy U.S. Coast Guard historian's office.)

The LORAN (Long Range Aid to Navigation) station at Folly Beach, shown in this c. 1960 photo, operated around the clock emitting electronic pulses seaward. Using the signals from the master station and two slave stations, ship navigators could get a fix for the exact location of their vessels. When the station was commissioned in March 1945, no publicity was given because the principles of LORAN were one of the service's carefully guarded secrets and were of vital use in navigation against the enemy. The station remained operational until its closing in December 1980. (Official U.S. Coast Guard photograph, courtesy U.S. Coast Guard historian's office.)

In this c. 1940s photo, Charleston area stevedores are shown in the hold of a liberty ship pushing a draft of ammunition into the proper position for the oncoming hoist. (Official U.S. Coast Guard photograph, courtesy U.S. Coast Guard historian's office.)

Shown on a lift truck at the Port of Embarkation docks (the present-day North Charleston Terminal) is a fragmentation bomb rack developed by coast guard and army officers attached to that unit. The purpose of the rack was to simplify the handling of the highly explosive missiles with a maximum of safety. (Official U.S. Coast Guard photograph, courtesy U.S. Coast Guard historian's office.)

A 155-mm gun is lifted onto a vessel in this November 1951 photo.

A field of military vehicles (above) are lined up waiting to be placed on board (below) for shipment overseas in these c. 1950s photo.

These November 1951 photos show military equipment—155-mm guns and jeeps—as a major export through the port during that turbulent decade.

Armored vehicles await the heavy-lift cranes at the North Charleston Terminal *c.* 1952.

Army vehicles line up on an open storage apron at the North Charleston Terminal awaiting overseas shipment in this August 1955 photo. On the right is a truckload of tobacco arriving for storage and shipment.

This 1959 photo shows the Charleston City Marina when it was the Navy Mine Craft Base. The brick building at the far right is the West Point Rice Mill. The marina in the background is now a lake. (Official U.S. Coast Guard photograph, courtesy U.S. Coast Guard historian's office.)

The helicopter shown in this May 1984 photo is being loaded aboard the Dart Lines *Americana* at the Wando-Welch Terminal en route to England. The aircraft is one of four British military anti-submarine crafts just back from trial runs in the Bahamas.

In this c. 1944 photo, the USS *Yorktown* pulls alongside the USS *Wasp* somewhere in the Pacific. (U.S. Navy photograph.)

The USS *Yorktown* is in posed formation with her escorts and some of her aircraft during Exercise Sea Imp, a major Southeast Asia Treaty Organization exercise conducted in the western Pacific during early 1966. (U.S. Navy photograph.)

Located in Charleston Harbor, Patriot's Point is home to the USS *Yorktown* (CV-10). The first *Yorktown* (CV-5) sank at the Battle of Midway. Moored next to the *Yorktown* at Patriot's Point is the USS *Laffey*, a World War II destroyer. Also alongside are the diesel attack submarine USS *Clamagore* and the U.S. Coast Guard cutter *Ingham*. Patriot's Point also highlights a carrier aviation hall of fame (shown below).

These are two of several warplanes on display at the Patriot's Point Museum.

After the base realignment closure of 1995, which moved most of the naval commands out of the Charleston area, several companies moved into facilities that previously housed the navy. Charleston Marine Containers Inc. (CMCI) was one such company. CMCI's products—mini containers that can be used as mobile warehouses for military deployments—are manufactured in North Charleston and shipped out to army, navy, and marine units.

When connected together, the mini containers form a standard 20-foot container. They are manufactured in two sizes—either "Quadcon" (in which four together equal a 20-foot container) or "Tricon" (in which three together equal a 20-foot container).

A Quadcon is moved into the cargo hold of a U.S. Air Force C-17 plane destined for Afghanistan.

A shipment of Tricons arrives at the Wando-Welch Terminal ready for export to the Middle East.

An M-1 tank rolls onto a Wallenius vessel at the North Charleston Terminal. The shipment is moved through Charleston by the Military Traffic Management Command and the Military Sealift Command, both working with the Department of Defense to bring supplies to combat units.

The LMSR (large, medium-speed Ro/Ro) vessels are instrumental in supplying military command teams, particularly during wartime. An entire brigade team—a fighting force capable of sustaining itself—can fit onto two LMSRs. The heavy-equipment transport C-17 planes based out of Charleston would have to make 400 trips to transport the same amount of equipment as two LMSRs.

The LMSR vessel USS *Watkins* discharges cargo from Afghanistan at the TC Dock in October 2002. The containers on the trailer were manufactured by CMCI.

Despite the closure of the naval facilities and shipyard, Charleston remains an important factor in military readiness. In coordination with the Military Traffic Management Command, the port recently helped move 14 Chinook helicopters, 7 Blackhawk helicopters, and a large number of other military vehicles through the North Charleston Terminal.

Five

ORGANIZING

MARITIME TRADE

After the Civil War, South Carolina's ports suffered economically and continued a downward spiral through World War I. Part of the problem was the state's inability to compete with rail freights in neighboring states. (Protests from the city's elite against rail lines coming into Charleston were largely to blame for the dilemma.)

In addition, there were several natural disasters—wharf fires, major hurricanes, and an earthquake—that caused significant damage to the ports.

In the 1920s, Charleston mayor John Grace led the City into purchasing the Charleston Terminal Company (which operated most of the port activities in Charleston) and forming the Public Utilities Commission (PUC). The PUC, funded through municipal bonds, got off to a fine start, and the dollar value of cargo moving through Charleston at that time doubled. However, by the end of the decade, the Great Depression would severely cripple the agency.

During World War II, state leaders realized the need to develop the port. In 1942, the general assembly created the South Carolina State Ports Authority, which took over management from the PUC and mandated development of ports in Charleston, Georgetown, and Port Royal.

After the war, the Ports Authority received the Army Port of Embarkation, which became the North Charleston Terminal, along with the docks in downtown Charleston, which became the Union Pier Terminal and the Columbus Street Terminal. The Ports Authority upgraded the facilities with new, modern equipment and set up sales offices in New York.

After taking over responsibility for the Georgetown port, the Ports Authority deepened the Winyah Bay channel to 27 feet, which helped improve shipping access. In 1959, the State Ports Authority declared Port Royal an active port and provided the necessary funding to dredge the basin and build transit sheds and berthing space.

Through the 1960s and 1970s, the port terminals were upgraded and expanded, the channel was dredged several times, and cranes were replaced periodically to keep up with the needs of the shipping companies. In 1966, Charleston received her first container shipment, and because the box could go from ship to truck easily, the intermodal era was born. In the 1980s, the Wando-Welch Terminal was built east of the Cooper as a dedicated container facility.

In 1999, the Ports Authority began studying the possibility of another containerport on Daniel Island. East of the Cooper residents came out in force against the proposal, citing quality of life issues. The Ports Authority backed down and later received approval from the state legislature to expand facilities on the southern end of the former navy base near existing rail lines.

While Georgetown and Port Royal continue to be used as bulk and breakbulk ports—and the Veterans Terminal promises to be a world-class bulk, breakbulk, and project cargo facility—Charleston is recognized today as the fourth largest containerport in the Southeast and the second most productive port in the world.

Sen. Strom Thurmond was a strong advocate of South Carolina's ports, and in the 1940s when he was governor, he helped establish the State Ports Authority. In the first volume and first issue of the organization's monthly publication, Thurmond wrote in the editorial, "South Carolina has awakened to the industrial and commercial significance of its seaboard location." He remained devoted to the growth of the state's ports until his death in June 2003.

This aerial view of the Union Pier Terminal, Charleston's first breakbulk terminal, was taken c. 1960s. The area at the top left part of the photo is the location of the present-day waterfront park. The terminal's location, just minutes from the Atlantic Ocean, gives it one of the fastest turn-around times of any seaport in the United States.

The Columbus Street Terminal is a general cargo facility handling container, breakbulk, and heavy-lift cargo. The past few decades have seen a sharp increase in container cargo, which has required several renovations of the terminal's facilities in order to accommodate the container traffic.

This July 1965 photo shows construction at a warehouse near the Union Pier Terminal. The building on the left (across Concord Street from the warehouse) is the U.S. Customs House. St. Philip's Episcopal Church is visible on the far right.

In November 1963, expansions at the Columbus Street Terminal included this dock extension.

Proximity to the navy base gives the North Charleston Terminal a mix of commercial and military customers.

The Wando-Welch Terminal, located on the East Cooper side of the harbor, was built in the 1980s. The terminal is a state-of-the-art container facility able to service several ships simultaneously.

When the port of Georgetown, located 60 miles north of Charleston, was dredged to 27 feet in the channel, it opened the seaport to shipping worldwide. Georgetown's ability to provide bulk and breakbulk service is one of the Ports Authority's most valuable assets.

Georgetown has come a long way since the days of indigo and rice shipments. A great deal of the cargo moving through Georgetown is manufactured at the nearby steel mills.

A new berth was installed at Georgetown in October 2001. The extension added an additional 100 feet to the existing 500 feet on one of the piers, which provided better moorings for the larger ships now calling on the port.

Port Royal, located 70 miles south of Charleston, has also dredged to 27 feet to make her harbor navigable by ocean-going vessels. Port Royal handles bulk and breakbulk cargo.

Congress has allocated money several times to dredge Charleston Harbor in order to allow larger vessels into her waterways. As of 2002, the inner harbor was deepened to 45 feet and the entrance channel to 47 feet. The Army Corps of Engineers maintains a close watch on any environmental impacts of such activities.

Through the years, the Ports Authority has acquired bigger, faster, and better cranes to accommodate larger, wider vessels coming into Charleston. The cranes above and on the facing page, bottom, show how far the container arms can stretch across the vessels. The photo on the facing page, top, shows the difference in a standard crane (at right) and the super post-Panamax cranes. When boomed up, they rise 360 feet and reach out 197 feet from the edge of the dock. They are the first container cranes in the United States to feature 100 percent AC power (as opposed to the previously used diesel-electric cranes), a cleaner power source.

In 2003, the State allocated a portion of the former navy base for the Ports Authority to convert into a new terminal. Dubbed the Veterans Terminal, the facility offers 110 acres of open storage area with rail access, 90,000 square feet of warehouse space, and four piers. The Veterans Terminal will be dedicated to non-containerized cargo, giving Charleston an added advantage among the Southeastern seaboard ports.

The addition of the cruise terminal in the 1970s offered the Ports Authority an additional revenue stream. Cruises out of Charleston are becoming more popular, and several cruise lines now "homeport" out of Charleston.

In 1946, a 10,000-ton freighter, the *Nicaragua Victory*, smashed into the Grace Memorial Bridge and ripped out a section. The broken span was fixed, and 20 years later, another bridge, the Silas N. Pearman, was built across the Cooper River.

Because the existing bridges across the Cooper River have been determined functionally obsolete, a new bridge is being constructed. The road deck will be 200 feet above the median high tide mark, which will allow larger ships to reach the Wando-Welch Terminal, North Charleston Terminal, and Veterans Terminal.

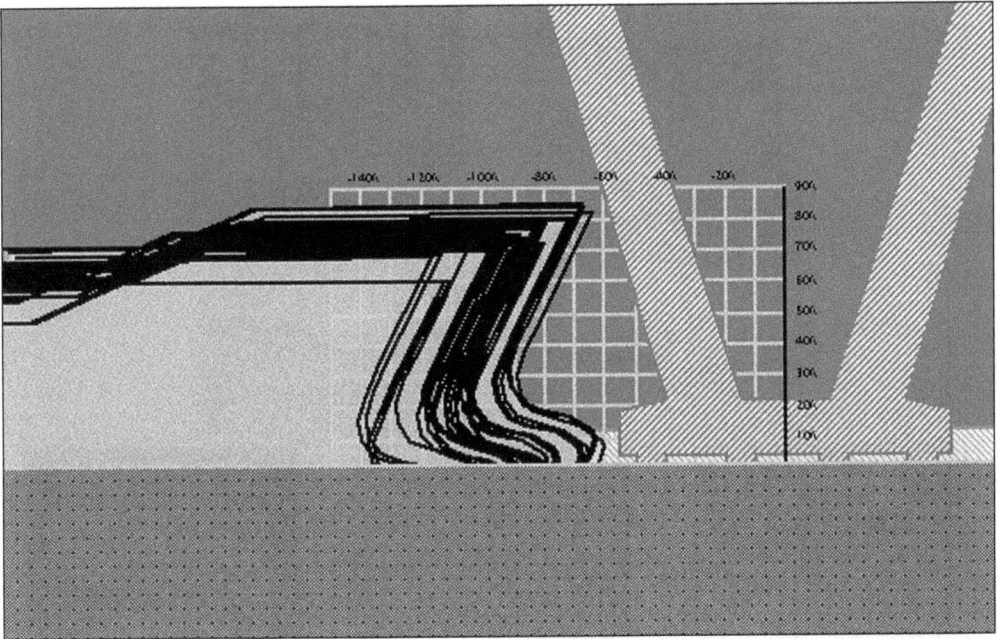

This illustration shows the rock islands at the base of the towers. On a footprint of five acres, each island is comprised of 12 shiploads of Newfoundland quarry stone, 3 shiploads of 160- to 300-pound pieces of armor stone, and 2 shiploads of 2400- to 4800-pound armor stones placed around the tower footings. This will force a ship to run aground before hitting the towers. (Drawing by Palmetto Bridge Constructors, courtesy South Carolina State Ports Authority.)

The drilled shafts supporting the main towers reach more than 230 feet below the waterline and into the earth. In comparison, from the waterline to the top of its trusses, the Pearman Bridge is only 285 feet high. (Drawing by Palmetto Bridge Constructors, courtesy South Carolina State Ports Authority.)

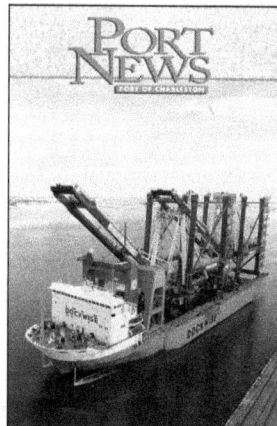

The covers of the Ports Authority's monthly magazine have reflected the changing emphases of the port throughout the years. From left to right beginning with the top row, the news at South Carolina's ports focused on bulk cargo (December 1947), military shipping (October 1957), heavy lift projects (February 1961), the cruise industry (April 1971), containerization (April 1985), container productivity (March 1994), and super-sized container cranes (October 2000).

Six

FORGING AN ECONOMIC MAGNET

In 1944, J.J. Pelley, president of the Association of American Railroads said, "Nothing will ever replace the old box-car." No one is questioning Mr. Pelley's wisdom or foresight, but it is obvious that Charleston didn't pay attention when she invested in containerization.

In the 1950s and 1960s, many of the manufacturing firms fled from the unions and high wages of the Northern states to South Carolina, where the anti-union, low-wage environment was more conducive to profits for the companies. The state also began recruiting companies from overseas, which exported goods through Charleston. These measures helped, but it was a simple six-sided box that helped ensure Charleston's position as a world-class port.

By the mid-1960s, the Ports Authority was purchasing additional waterfront property and enlarging berthing and storage facilities in preparation for the transformation of maritime commerce: the standardized shipping container. In 1966, the port handled its first standardized container, and it was as if Charleston had found her calling. During the 1960s and 1970s, shippers were able to reduce labor costs and improve efficiency by shipping with containers.

Containerization created a revolution in transporting goods. Today's container ships are larger than earlier ships, and containerized cargo can be unloaded more quickly than bulk cargo. With bulk and breakbulk cargo, several days were required to unload or load a ship. With containers, ships can be unloaded or loaded in hours.

Charleston has become one of the most efficient ports in the world, which experts say will draw container ships on a regular line of service.

Al Parish, an economist at Charleston Southern University, notes: "The port is one of the top three or four reasons manufacturers cite for locating to South Carolina. The port helps the state maintain manufacturing jobs that pay much more than service jobs and help bring up incomes for the working class." Trade through South Carolina's ports provides more than 83,000 jobs in South Carolina and pumps approximately $11 billion in sales into the state economy each year.

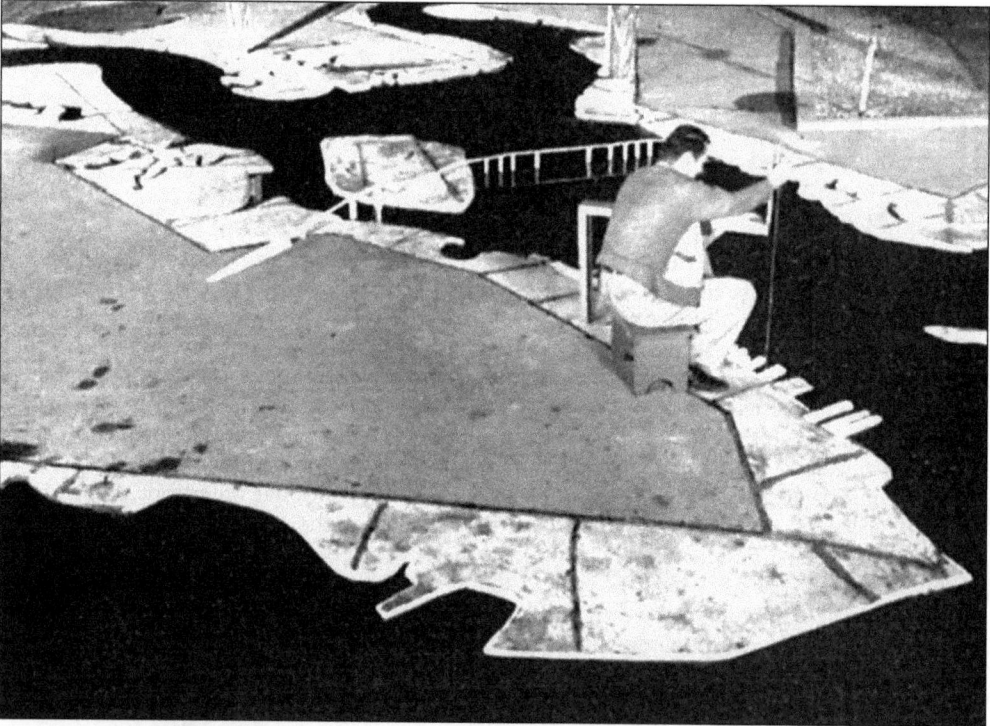

In 1949, Charleston Harbor was under study as a model harbor by the U.S. Engineers Waterways Experiment Station at Vicksburg, Mississippi. Reproduced to scale in a warehouse, the model included docks, piers, and water that simulates the regular tidal flow. The project helped the engineers study harbor maintenance and improvements to better serve growing port commerce.

Charleston Port Called 'Amazing'

ATLANTA, June 7. (AP): Charleston has forged ahead of Savannah in tonnage moved through the ports.

Exports from the Savannah port continued a downward trend in the first quarter of this year, dropping $17,500,000 from the figure for the corresponding period in 1947.

The figures, compiled by the U. S. department of commerce for the states ports authority, showed that the Georgia city's imports also fell off $2,120,000 for the comparative period.

For the first quarter, compared with the corresponding 1947 period, Charleston showed a $2,236,000 increase in exports and a $2,058,000 gain in imports.

During the past 27 months, the report showed, Savannah lost $107,-000,000 worth of export business while the South Carolina port gained $44,500,000.

Reports from other Southern ports also show gains since 1946 but none so "spectacular" as those of Charleston, the report added.

Harry G. Thornton, president of the newly organized Georgia Port Development association, attributed Charleston's "amazing revival" to acquisition of the $20,000,000 port of embarkation by the South Carolina State ports authority.

"Until Georgia ports become modernized like other Southern ports we can expect the downward export trend to continue," Thornton said.

He added that the port of Savannah has undergone little modernization since the early 1900's. Of the major Southern ports, all except Savannah are publicly owned and the Georgia port is the only one which has lost ground, he said.

Within a year after the formation of the State Ports Authority, Charleston was developing quite a reputation for being a productive seaport. More amazing than this headline was the fact that the news came out of Georgia—traditionally Charleston's closest and most fierce competitor.

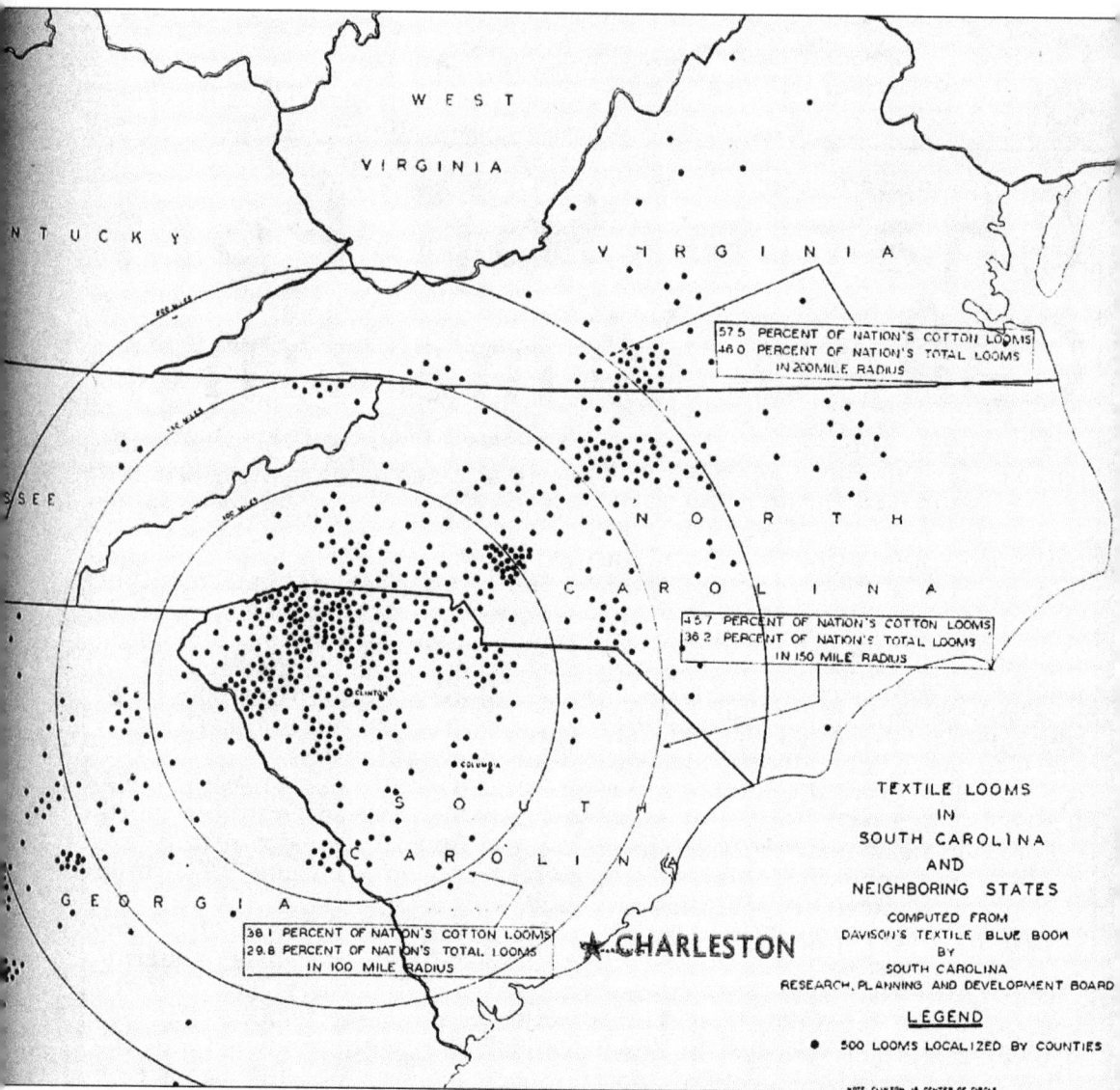

**TEXTILE LOOMS
IN
SOUTH CAROLINA
AND
NEIGHBORING STATES**

COMPUTED FROM
DAVISON'S TEXTILE BLUE BOOK
BY
SOUTH CAROLINA
RESEARCH, PLANNING AND DEVELOPMENT BOARD

LEGEND

● 500 LOOMS LOCALIZED BY COUNTIES

57.5 PERCENT OF NATION'S COTTON LOOMS
46.0 PERCENT OF NATION'S TOTAL LOOMS
IN 200 MILE RADIUS

45.7 PERCENT OF NATION'S COTTON LOOMS
36.2 PERCENT OF NATION'S TOTAL LOOMS
IN 150 MILE RADIUS

38.1 PERCENT OF NATION'S COTTON LOOMS
29.8 PERCENT OF NATION'S TOTAL LOOMS
IN 100 MILE RADIUS

★ CHARLESTON

In the 1940s and early 1950s, the existence of textile plants was a sure sign of growth in an area. This map shows the South Carolina Upstate teeming with textile facilities—mostly cotton.

Cotton made its way from the fields, shown in this undated photo (above) and eventually onto vessels (below) in Charleston, Georgetown, and Port Royal.

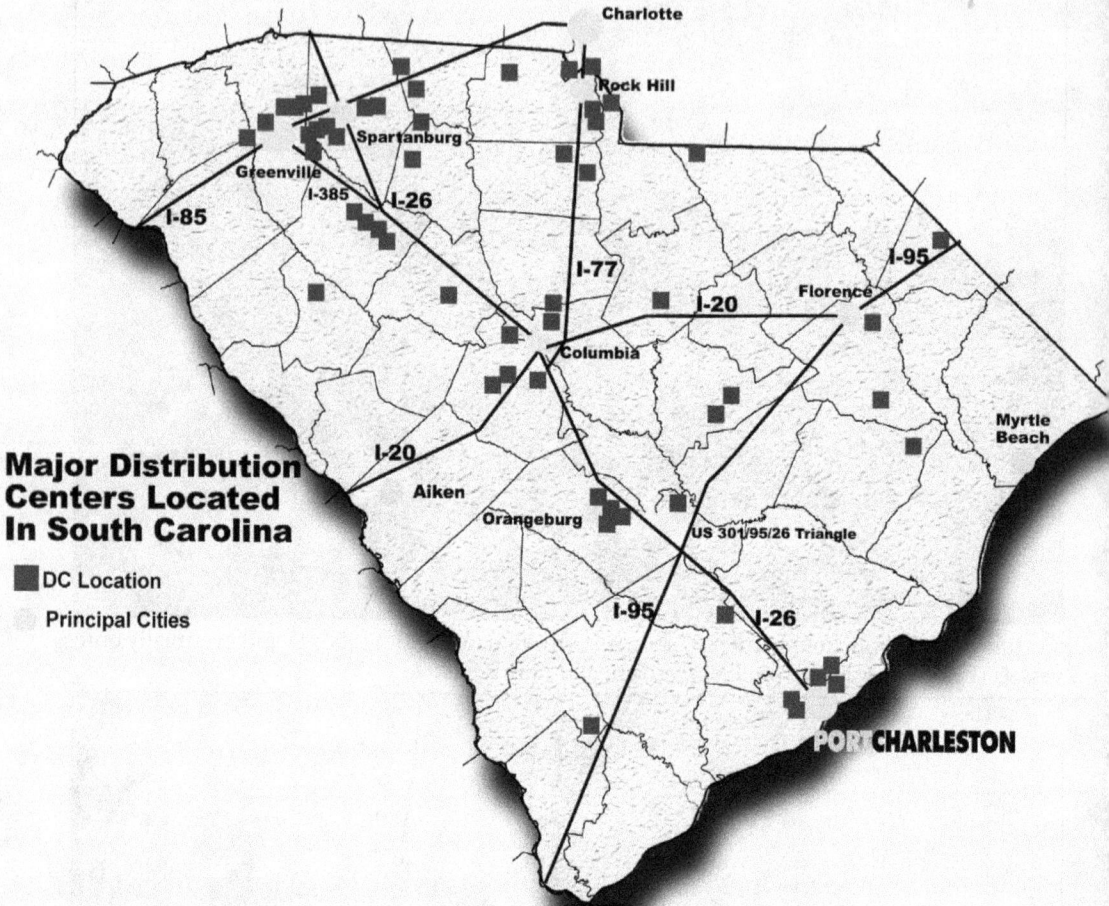

Major Distribution Centers Located In South Carolina

■ DC Location

○ Principal Cities

Map labels: Charlotte, Rock Hill, Spartanburg, Greenville, I-385, I-85, I-26, I-77, I-20, Columbia, Florence, I-95, Myrtle Beach, Aiken, Orangeburg, US 301/95/26 Triangle, I-95, I-26, PORT CHARLESTON

Containerization of goods has made distribution centers a sign of economic stability. The map above shows the location of distribution centers throughout the state. The distribution centers become a type of way station for the containers, which can be brought straight to the center from the ship. At the distribution centers, the goods are stored in warehouses, such as those on the facing page, or are unloaded, sorted, and reloaded into other containers for efficient transport to end users.

Times have changed, and South Carolina's ports have changed with them.

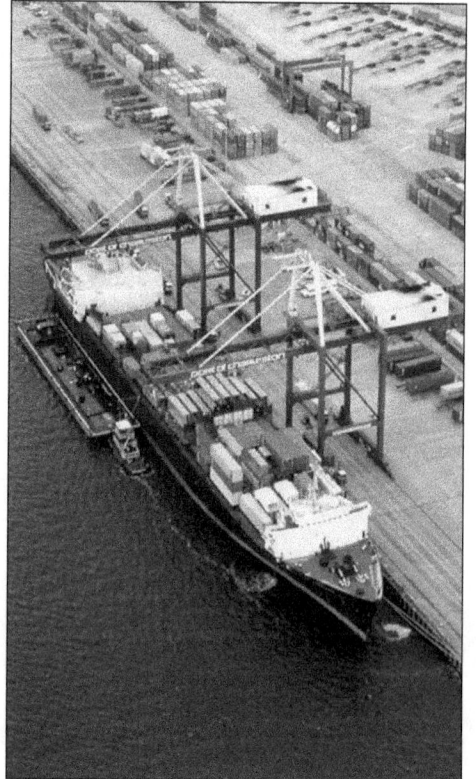

Whereas bulk cargo loading was once the primary activity at the docks, today most cargo is shipped in containers.

Importing and exporting automobiles is one area that has changed very little over the years. Only style and design have changed; the lots are still full of vehicles awaiting shipment.

These photos show the growth of Charleston's waterfront area over the years. The photo on the left is *c.* 1950; the photo on the right is *c.* 1998.

Note the increase in warehouses, container yards, and other industrial and commercial buildings in the more recent photo.

With the onset of containerization in the 1960s, the ports found a new way of planning and measuring shipping. Instead of figuring the pounds of chicken, steel, or cotton being shipped, the new measurement is TEUs—or twenty-foot equivalent unit. Because each container is a standard size, shipping is more easily calculated.

With the TEU calculation, measuring productivity became easier as well. If it takes "X" minutes to load one container, one worker should be able to move "Y" boxes in "Z" hours. Charleston did the math—and did it well. Today, Charleston is ranked second in the world (behind Hong Kong) in number of containers moved onto and off of ships.

Inland movement of cargo has also changed over the years. In the *c.* 1949 photo above, a rail line came up to the Union Pier Terminal behind the U.S. Customs House, where bulk cargo was loaded. The photo below shows the method of movement for most cargo today—containers shipped via truck.

Charleston's efficiency has flowed over into the trucking industry. With the ability to move containers quickly, truckers spent significantly less time waiting at the terminals. Charleston is known worldwide for having one of the fastest turn-times for trucks.

Tourism remains one of the area's most important economic draws. Most of Charleston's tourist-related activities center around the maritime areas, including the cruise terminal (above) and Waterfront Park (below).

Seven

SAFETY AND SECURITY

Charleston is no stranger to safety and security issues.

According to R.S. MacElwee's account, "The Port of Charleston, S.C." in *Official History of the Police Department of Charleston, S.C.* (Walker, Evans & Cogswell, 1928), on March 16, 1698, John Randolph, collector of the king's customs, reported:

Charles Towne is the safest port for all vessels coming through the Gulf of Florida in distress, bound from the West Indies to the Northern Plantations: if they miss this place they may perish at sea for want of relief, and having beat upon the coast of New England, New York, and Virginia by a North West Wind in the Winter be forced to go to Barbados if they miss this Bay where no wind will damage them and all things will be had necessary to refit them.

Despite this rousing endorsement, Charleston, Georgetown, and Port Royal had to deal with both safety issues, which necessitated the lighthouses dotting the coast, and security issues, namely Blackbeard, Stede Bonnet, and other pirates of the day.

Through the years, safety and security in the harbors were managed by the U.S. Coast Guard with assistance from the navy and other military agencies. The attacks of September 11 brought the issue to the forefront, and once again, Charleston stepped forward to set the pace.

Project Seahawk, the nation's first port security command and control center, is a unique intermodal transportation and port security pilot project that began in Charleston in March 2003. The project is a comprehensive effort to coordinate the port security responsibilities of the various federal, state, local, and private entities charged with defending the Port of Charleston.

Project Seahawk brings these agencies together under one port security command center and functions proactively in the intermodal transportation link and the port environment to act as a deterrent. The Seahawk center combines intermodal transportation and harbor security data—including video camera feeds, radar, and thermal imaging—along with information about crews and cargo, to assess any potential threat by that vessel.

Even in its early stages, Project Seahawk was showing signs of success. In April 2003, only a month after its inception, a federal task force working with Project Seahawk rounded up 35 suspected illegal aliens near the Cooper River Bridge construction site. The incident was the first operation conducted by the task force, which investigates suspicious containers, cargo, vessels, boats, barges, events, people, and businesses that may pose a threat to the port.

An added advantage of piloting Project Seahawk in Charleston is the availability of facilities for training. Charleston is already home to the Border Patrol Academy, which is being converted into a federal law enforcement training center.

The Morris Island Lighthouse still stands as a reminder of safety for ocean-going vessels.

These c. 1916 photos show the U.S. Coast Guard's lighthouse depot under construction. (Photos from the collection of Sedgwick L. Simons, courtesy U.S. Coast Guard historian's office.)

The Charleston Port Security Force firefighters are shown in a c. 1940 photo during one of their weekly drills along the U.S. Navy Fleet landing. The U.S. Customs House on East Bay Street is visible in the background. (Official U.S. Coast Guard photograph, courtesy U.S. Coast Guard historian's office.)

The U.S. Coast Guard mounted horse patrols, shown in this c. 1940 photo, closely coordinated land and sea patrols in the vigil for enemy spies and saboteurs. The headquarters for the coast guard's mounted beach patrol was located with the captain of the port in Charleston. In North Charleston, there was a mounted beach patrol training station, and on James Island, dogs were trained at a coast guard station to perform sentry duty for the armed forces. (Official U.S. Coast Guard photograph, courtesy U.S. Coast Guard historian's office.)

Fireboats of the Port Security Office are shown on October 6, 1944, fighting a fire at the Southern Railway Pier. Charleston Fire Department officials credited the coast guard for keeping damages to a minimum. The Cooper River Bridge can be seen in the background. (Official U.S. Coast Guard photograph, courtesy U.S. Coast Guard historian's office.)

In this c. 1940s photo, chains, mooring blocks, and buoys stand ready for use on the pier at the repair base at the foot of Tradd Street. A coast guard air-sea rescue crash boat, three buoy tenders, and a lightship are moored along the L-shaped pier. (Official U.S. Coast Guard photograph, courtesy U.S. Coast Guard historian's office.)

On the night of September 21, 1989, Hurricane Hugo roared through Charleston, leaving behind a path of destruction. Among the casualties were toppled containers and cranes.

Even in the midst of cleanup of its damaged equipment, the Ports Authority assisted the community by providing its cruise terminal as a warehouse for food and supplies.

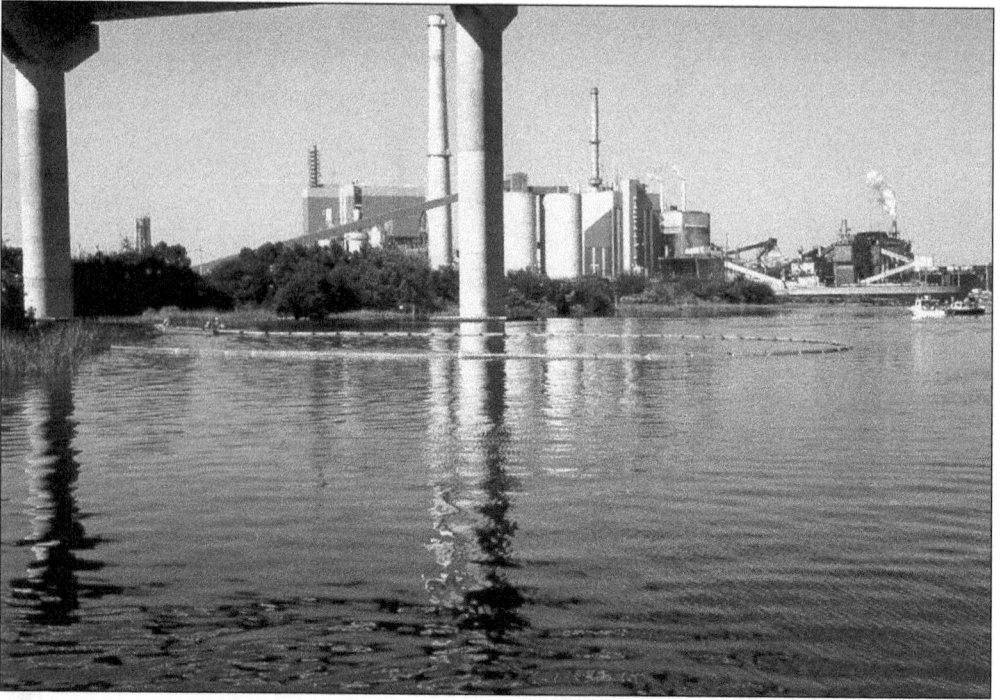

A containment boom, used by Turecamo Environmental Services to assist in oil spills, is deployed during a multi-contractor drill in the waters near North Charleston.

Several booms are pre-positioned for rapid deployment in the event of an oil spill.

118

Workers at the Ports Authority undergo safety training several times throughout the year.

Among the mandatory safety rules is a harness, hard hat, and steel-toed shoes.

This flag was hoisted above the tallest crane at the Columbus Street Terminal following the September 11 attacks.

Random inspections were already being performed before September 11. Afterward, the inspections increased, although most truckers took the delays in stride.

Before September 11, the focus for port police officers was safety. After the attacks, it was safety *and* security.

Port Police Chief Lindy Rinaldi remarked after the attacks that she knew her job had always been important; what changed was seeing how significant the effects of what she does can be. The World Trade Center in New York housed the New York/New Jersey Ports Authority and the Port Police. Some of those who died were Rinaldi's colleagues and friends.

B.J., the Ports Authority's only police dog, is man's—and security's—best friend. After graduation from the K-9 Academy, B.J. joined the force to sniff out drugs and explosives. Most often on foot patrol, B.J. and his handler also work on security for the cruise ships.

For cargo transport and personnel safety, heightened security, which includes both air and sea patrols for the U.S. Coast Guard, is the order of the day.

A police boat patrols beside a demonstration of a "drone" watercraft manipulated by remote control. (Photo by Brad Nettles; courtesy *Post and Courier*.)

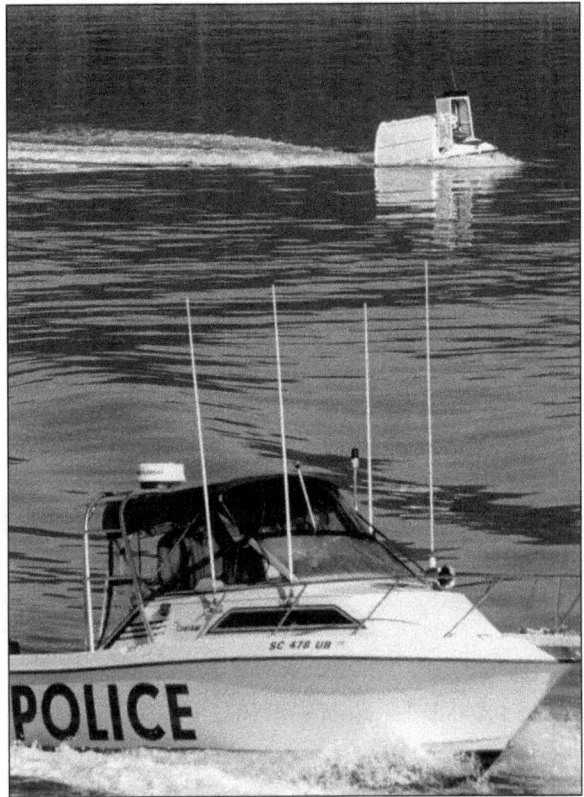

U.S. Customs has implemented a new vehicle and cargo inspection system (VACIS), which X-rays containers to detect the presence of drugs or weapons.

During a 2003 visit to Charleston, Sen. Lindsey Graham (center) reviews port security at the Wando-Welch Terminal with then-Charleston customs director Julian Miller (left) and Chief Inspector Bill Ratliff.

Federal officials are briefed on port security by customs supervisor Blondell Hayes (front right) during a visit to Charleston in 2002. From left to right are Commissioner of Customs and Border Protection Robert Bonner, Sen. Ernest F. Hollings (D-SC), Sen. John Breaux (D-LA), and Adm. James Loy, commandant of the U.S. Coast Guard. (Photo by Brad Nettles; courtesy *Post and Courier*.)

During his visit to Charleston in 2004, President Bush chose Union Pier as the location to highlight the importance of port security efforts. Charleston was selected to spearhead Project Seahawk, the nation's first port security command and control center.

The sheriff's patrol boat assists in port security maneuvers. Under Project Seahawk, 47 different agencies work together for the common goal of safety and security along the waterfront.

Patrolman Phillip Shuler (left) and Sgt. Roger Cishek, both of the Port Police, keep watch while a cruise ship is at dock.